A TRUE BOOK

Extreme Places
The Highest and the Lowest

KATIE MARSICO

Children's Press®
An Imprint of Scholastic Inc.

Content Consultant
Injeong Jo, PhD
Assistant Professor
Department of Geography
Texas State University
San Marcos, Texas

Library of Congress Cataloging-in-Publication Data
Marsico, Katie, 1980– author.
The highest and the lowest / by Katie Marsico.
    pages cm. — (A true book)
 Summary: "Learn all about the highest and lowest places on Earth and find out what it takes for life to survive in these extreme locations." — Provided by publisher.
 Includes bibliographical references and index.
 ISBN 978-0-531-21723-8 (library binding : alk. paper) — ISBN 978-0-531-21788-7 (pbk. : alk. paper)
 1. Physical geography—Juvenile literature. 2. Altitudes—Juvenile literature. 3. Climatic extremes—Juvenile literature. 4. Everest, Mount (China and Nepal)—Juvenile literature. 5. Mariana Trench—Juvenile literature. I. Title. II. Series: True book.
 GB58.M37 2016
 551.8—dc23   2015010674

All rights reserved. Published in 2016 by Children's Press, an imprint of Scholastic Inc.
Printed in the United States of America 113
SCHOLASTIC, CHILDREN'S PRESS, A TRUE BOOK™, and associated logos are trademarks and/or registered trademarks of Scholastic Inc.
1 2 3 4 5 6 7 8 9 10 R 25 24 23 22 21 20 19 18 17 16

Front cover (main): The _DEEPSEA CHALLENGER_ descending toward the Challenger Deep

Front cover (Inset): A climber on Mount Everest

Back cover: Sir Edmund Hillary and Tenzing Norgay on Mount Everest

Find the Truth!

Everything you are about to read is true *except* for one of the sentences on this page.

Which one is **TRUE**?

T or F   Mount Everest is Earth's tallest mountain.

T or F   Deep within the TauTona mine, temperatures are extremely hot.

Find the answers in this book.

Contents

THE BIG TRUTH!

Bar-headed goose

Extreme Adapters

4

La Rinconada is the highest human settlement in the world.

Lights on miners' helmets help them
see when deep below Earth's surface.

5

Mount Everest is located on the border between China and Nepal.

From Icy Peaks to Dark Waters

Rising high in the Himalaya mountain range, Mount Everest is Earth's highest point. Every so often, the peak's icy stillness is interrupted by troops of daring climbers. Most people only attempt to scale Everest when equipped with an emergency supply of oxygen. At such a high **elevation,** the air is thinner and contains less of this essential gas. Even the boldest adventurers realize that Everest represents a magnificent but potentially deadly extreme.

Highs and Lows

While Everest is Earth's highest point above sea level, the Challenger Deep lies at the opposite extreme. Located in the Mariana **Trench** in the Pacific Ocean, it is the lowest point on Earth's surface. The trench lies miles beneath the waves. To explore it, scientists face crushing water pressure, total darkness, and freezing temperatures. They have therefore relied on robotic technology to unlock the many mysteries of the Challenger Deep.

Missions to the depths of the ocean have led to the discovery of fascinating animal species, such as this chimaera, a distant relative of sharks.

People have built homes and other buildings in surprisingly high places. The Taktsang Palphug Monastery in the Himalayas sits more than 10,000 feet (3,000 m) above sea level.

It's not only adventurous climbers and underwater robots that encounter extreme heights and depths. Tens of thousands of people live in cities built in high places. Others work in gold mines deep below Earth's surface. In all these situations, people must cope with the challenges and dangers that go hand in hand with their extreme circumstances.

Le Morne Brabant on the island of Mauritius rises more than 1,800 feet (550 m) above sea level.

Fortunately, people and other organisms have developed ways to **adapt** to such extremes. To understand how and why they do this, it is important to know exactly what elevation means. Elevation is the distance from sea level of an object or place on Earth's surface. Sea level is the average height of the surface of the sea.

Changes in elevation frequently bring changes in the **atmosphere**. This means that weather, water pressure, and air pressure tend to be different at different heights and depths. People don't always notice these variations if they only experience slight shifts in elevation. With extreme shifts, however, they must prepare for greater changes in the atmosphere—and greater risks and physical side effects.

Do your ears ever pop when you fly in an airplane? That's because the air pressure is rapidly changing as the plane flies higher or lower.

All of Earth's 10 highest mountains are in the Himalayas.

CHAPTER 2

Atop Earth's Highest Point

Nicknamed Mother Goddess of the Earth by local people, Mount Everest is surely the best-known of the Himalaya mountains. This spectacular range stretches across China, Nepal, India, Pakistan, Bhutan, and Afghanistan. Everest is located in the eastern Himalayas. The mountain looms more than 29,000 feet (8,800 m) above sea level. That's about 5.5 miles, more than 15 times the average height of the world's tallest skyscrapers!

Mount Everest

Highest or Tallest?

Mount Everest is described as Earth's highest point. Yet Everest is not, in fact, the tallest mountain in the world. That distinction goes to Mauna Kea, a volcano on the island of Hawaii. Mauna Kea measures nearly 33,000 feet (10,000 m) tall, but roughly 60 percent of it lies underwater, or below sea level. As a result, Everest's peak towers farther above sea level than that of the volcano.

Because much of its height is hidden underwater, Mauna Kea does not appear as high as other large mountains.

Special cold-weather gear, such as waterproof clothing and oxygen masks, are necessary for survival on Mount Everest.

An Extreme Climate

With the sky-high elevation around Everest's summit comes a severe climate. In winter, wind speeds sometimes reach 175 miles (282 kilometers) per hour. On warmer days, the temperature generally doesn't climb above 15 degrees Fahrenheit (–9.4 degrees Celsius). In addition, there is 33 percent less oxygen near Everest's summit than is present at sea level.

Animals such as the bharal, a type of sheep, are a common sight in parts of the Himalayas.

Survival Near the Summit

A wide range of wildlife exists close to Mount Everest's base. Yet few organisms are able to endure the extreme conditions nearer to the summit. Certain birds such as bar-headed geese have been spotted **migrating** through this harsh environment. For the most part, however, animals do not remain in the area for long. At elevations greater than 19,000 feet (5,800 m), plants cannot grow on Everest.

For mountain climbers, reaching the summit of Mount Everest is a challenging test of the limits of human endurance. Falling, freezing, lack of oxygen, and avalanches all pose severe threats to adventurers. Many have died while attempting to reach the summit. New Zealander Edmund Hillary and Nepalese Sherpa Tenzing Norgay were the first to successfully reach the top. They completed their historic climb in 1953.

Edmund Hillary (left) and Tenzing Norgay (right) made history with their amazing journey to the peak of Mount Everest.

As a precaution, most people trying to scale Mount Everest hire trained guides to assist them on their journey. Supplies for this climb include everything from ice axes to walkie-talkies and oxygen masks. It typically takes six to nine weeks to arrive at the summit. The length of time depends on weather conditions and climbers' skill levels. The costs for such a trip are staggering. They range from $30,000 to $100,000 per person!

A team of mountain climbers poses at the summit of Mount Everest.

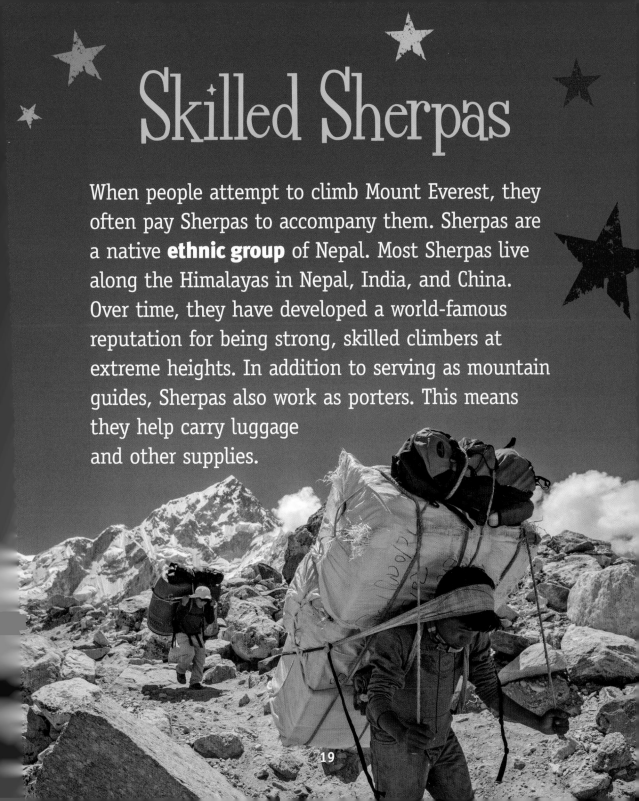

Skilled Sherpas

When people attempt to climb Mount Everest, they often pay Sherpas to accompany them. Sherpas are a native **ethnic group** of Nepal. Most Sherpas live along the Himalayas in Nepal, India, and China. Over time, they have developed a world-famous reputation for being strong, skilled climbers at extreme heights. In addition to serving as mountain guides, Sherpas also work as porters. This means they help carry luggage and other supplies.

This illustration shows the topography, or landscape, of the ocean and land around the Mariana Trench. Red and orange indicate the highest areas. Lower regions range from green to blue to purple.

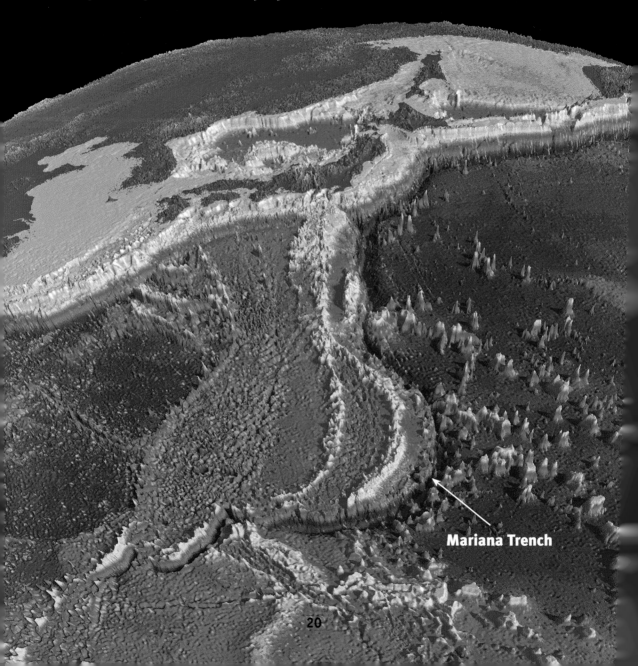

Mariana Trench

The Deepest of the Deep

Just how deep is the Mariana Trench? To get a sense of this, imagine dropping Mount Everest into the trench's deepest point. If you could accomplish that, Everest's peak would still be underwater. In fact, there would be a 1-mile (1.6 km) gap between the mountaintop and the surface of the Pacific Ocean. That's because the trench's deepest point lies 6.8 miles (11 km) beneath the waves. This point is known as the Challenger Deep.

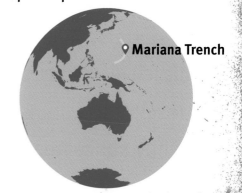

Mariana Trench

The Mariana Trench is named after the nearby Mariana Islands in the western Pacific Ocean.

Into the Deep

The Challenger Deep is nearly 36,000 feet (11,000 m) beneath the ocean's surface. It is shaped almost entirely by extreme conditions. For starters, sunlight doesn't reach that deep. This leaves the area cloaked in darkness. As a result, the water's temperature hovers only slightly above freezing.

In addition, water pressure increases with depth. In the Challenger Deep, water pressure is more than 1,000 times the pressure at sea level. Experts compare it to the weight of 50 jumbo jets! What life can exist in such conditions? Scientists hope to answer this by exploring the Challenger Deep.

Deep-sea submersibles such as the *DEEPSEA CHALLENGER* are designed to withstand intense water pressure and other extreme conditions.

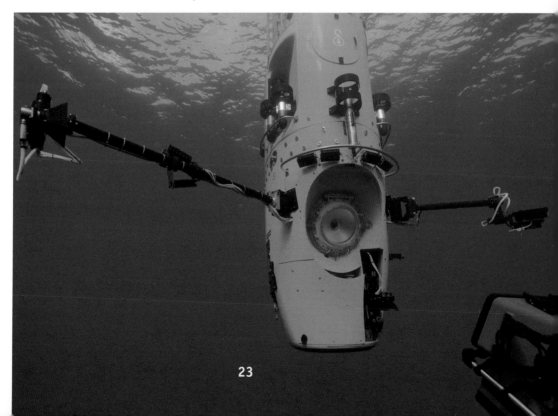

Mysteries of the Deep

Researchers first discovered the Challenger Deep in 1875. Since then, people have been eager to learn more about life there. Since the mid-20th century, they have used technology including **sonar** and, more recently, robotic **probes** to explore this area. Scientists have also traveled there in submarines. Along the way, they have collected samples of seawater and organisms to analyze. With each voyage, researchers piece together more information about the mysteries of the Challenger Deep.

In 1960, the *Trieste* became the first submersible ever to reach the bottom of the Challenger Deep.

Scientists have learned about life in the Challenger Deep by collecting samples and taking photos on deep-sea expeditions.

So far, scientists have learned that the Challenger Deep is home to hundreds of simple organisms. These include **microbes** and shrimplike animals called amphipods. The cells of these tiny creatures appear to have unusually flexible membranes, or linings. This may help them tolerate the crushing water pressure of extreme depths. Further research will help scientists learn more about this and other mysteries of life in the deep ocean.

Extreme Adapters

Super-high elevations and super-low depths pose challenges for animals as well as for people. The creatures that do manage to live at these extremes show adaptations that help them survive.

Ocean-Floor Feeders
Sea pigs are related to starfish. They live as deep as 3.7 miles (6 km) beneath the ocean's surface, where food can be scarce. Sea pigs rely on their tubelike feet to search for—and devour—tiny pieces of rotting plant and animal matter on the ocean floor.

High-Elevation Spiders

Himalayan jumping spiders have been found on Mount Everest at elevations as high as 22,000 feet (6,700 m). Few other organisms survive at this height. These predator spiders feed on tiny insects in the air, whipped by the wind toward the mountain's summit.

Fast-Breathing Birds

Bar-headed geese must survive the harsh environment high on Everest when they migrate. At high altitudes, they breathe more than seven times faster than at sea level. This fast breathing enables them to get enough oxygen—but would make humans dizzy.

Deep-Cave Dwellers

Most people would never notice tiny springtails—especially the species that live in the utter darkness roughly 1.2 miles (1.9 km) underground. These darkness-dwelling insects lack eyes. They rely instead on special sensory cells. These cells detect chemical signals that give them information about the environment.

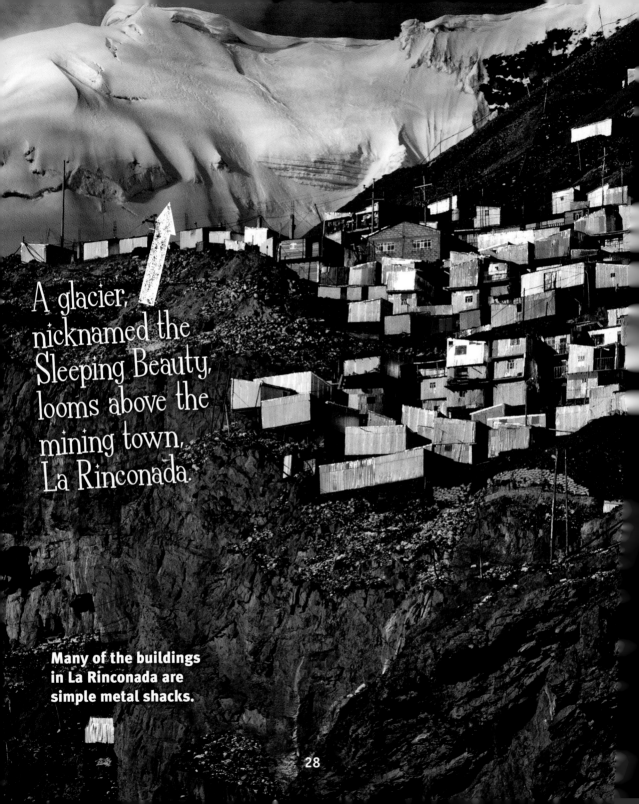

A glacier, nicknamed the Sleeping Beauty, looms above the mining town, La Rinconada.

Many of the buildings in La Rinconada are simple metal shacks.

CHAPTER 4

A City in the Sky

New visitors to La Rinconada, Peru, shouldn't be surprised if they feel dizzy or short of breath. These are symptoms of altitude sickness, a condition that can affect people at extremely high elevations. Yet long-term residents of La Rinconada generally don't suffer from it. They have adapted to conditions there. Roughly 30,000 people are members of this mining community. At almost 17,000 feet (5,200 m), it is the highest city in the world.

La Rinconada, Peru

Most miners make very little money, despite the hard work and harsh conditions in the mines.

The Lure of Gold

La Rinconada is located in the Andes Mountains. This South American range spans Ecuador, Chile, Colombia, Peru, Argentina, Bolivia, and Venezuela. La Rinconada may be famous for its extreme elevation, but that's not why people go there. Most residents came to work in the nearby gold mine.

Without the lure of gold, it's doubtful such a large community would ever have developed there. So high up in the Andes, La Rinconada is remote, or far from populated areas. People must travel along steep, isolated roads to reach the city. La Rinconada's extreme elevation also brings a harsh climate. Bad weather frequently leaves passageways into the city coated in ice.

Traveling to and from La Rinconada is difficult, and few people make the journey very often.

31

An additional challenge for the city's residents is pollution. In general, air pollution tends to be greater at higher elevations. In La Rinconada, where mining operations contaminate the air, pollution has become an especially serious problem. Local mining operations rely on toxic, or poisonous, chemicals such as mercury, which are regularly released into the atmosphere.

Workers mix mined rock with mercury to separate the rock from precious gold flecks.

A pair of miners sit on a ledge overlooking La Rinconada.

Adapting to La Rinconada

For the people of La Rinconada, these harsh conditions are a part of day-to-day life. Unlike visitors who scale Mount Everest, city residents cope with the high elevation on a long-term basis. It's impractical for them to continually carry an extra supply of oxygen wherever they go. Fortunately, the citizens of La Rinconada have developed certain physical adaptations. These help them survive in their extreme environment.

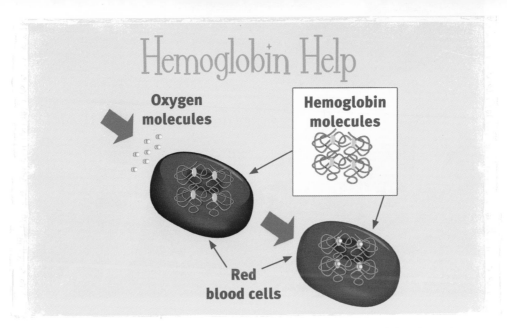

Hemoglobin Help

Oxygen attaches to hemoglobin in blood cells. As the blood cells move through the body, the oxygen is carried along with them.

Special Blood Cells

Visitors to La Rinconada sometimes struggle with its thinner air and decreased oxygen levels. Yet residents usually do not. Their ability to breathe more easily is related to adaptations within their red blood cells. People living high up in the Andes tend to have more hemoglobin in their blood. Hemoglobin is a protein that helps carry oxygen throughout a person's body.

Residents of La Rinconada don't breathe any faster or harder than anyone else. Yet their increased hemoglobin levels allow them to breathe more efficiently. Of course, people in La Rinconada still must cope with a harsh climate and the effects of pollution. Over time, however, their bodies have adapted to at least one extreme challenge in the world's highest city.

Because of the city's isolation, there are no services to remove trash from La Rinconada.

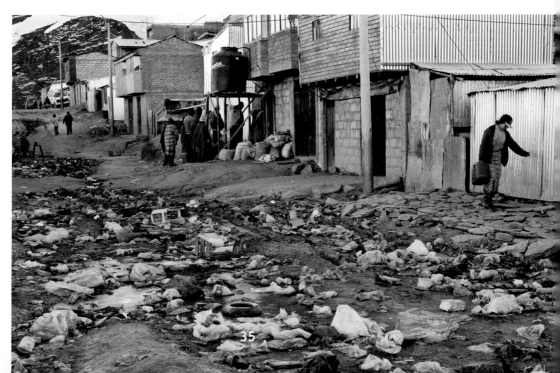

TauTona is home to rich
deposits of gold.

CHAPTER 5

Lowered Into the Lion's Mouth

Just as humans follow gold to Earth's highest reaches, they also follow it into its lowest depths. Since 1962, gold miners in South Africa have been descending into the mouth of TauTona, or the "Great Lion." *TauTona*, from the African Setswana language, is the name of the world's deepest mine in operation. Every day, workers at TauTona make a risky journey 2.4 miles (3.9 km) beneath the surface of the earth.

TauTona mine, South Africa

Dangers in the Depths

TauTona is located in western Gauteng, a province in South Africa. The mine produces hundreds of millions of dollars worth of gold each year. Approximately 5,600 miners work there doing a job that is neither easy nor safe. For starters, laborers at TauTona must take a dangerous trip deep into the earth to reach the mine. They spend much of this journey in a lift cage, which is similar to an elevator car.

After descending miles down in an elevator, miners ride underground trains to the tunnels where they'll be working.

Mining gold requires hard physical labor, which is made even more difficult by the hot, cramped conditions of TauTona.

The miners' ride down to the deepest parts of TauTona generally lasts about an hour. Because rock and air temperatures both increase with depth, the work environment is blisteringly hot. The face of the rock within the mine is 140°F (60°C)! As a result, miners are at risk of suffering from a condition called heatstroke.

The extremely high value of gold makes gold mining big business—despite difficult conditions for workers.

Heatstroke occurs when extreme heat raises a person's body temperature to 104°F (40°C) or greater. If untreated, heatstroke damages the brain, heart, kidneys, and muscles. Severe cases can even lead to death. Additional dangers at TauTona include falling rock, which has proven deadly in the past. When accidents happen, the mine's extreme depth makes rescue efforts both slow and difficult.

Keeping Mining Safe

To stay safe, miners keep certain supplies within close reach at all times. For example, miners wear helmets to protect their heads from falling rocks. Miners also typically have access to an emergency breathing pack. The pack provides about 30 minutes' worth of oxygen. This is especially important because some underground areas feature decreased oxygen levels or natural gases that make people sick.

Cooling the Mine

Mine operators have taken various measures to combat extreme conditions at TauTona. For example, they use air-conditioning equipment to cool the mine. Most of the time, this keeps the air temperature at about 82°F (28°C). Nevertheless, accidents continue to claim an average of five lives a year at TauTona. Workers there—and in underground mines across the globe—still face significant risks by descending to extreme depths.

Rescue workers help a young miner to safety after rescuing him from a collapsed mine in Nicaragua in 2014.

As long as there are heights to scale and depths to explore, people will continue working to reach the planet's most extreme elevations.

Amazing Extremes

From the harsh conditions of La Rinconada to those of TauTona, extreme heights and depths have a big impact on how people work and live. Such extremes are also an ongoing source of fascination. Adventurers still climb Mount Everest's frozen summit. Scientists remain intrigued by the mysteries of the Challenger Deep. Though they often involve struggles and risks, such extreme elevations help shape the world. And in response to them, people and other organisms continue exploring, adapting, and surviving. ★

True Statistics

Height of Mount Everest: 29,029 ft. (8,800 m) above sea level

Elevation beyond which no plants grow on Everest: 19,000 ft. (5,800 m) above sea level

Depth of the Challenger Deep: 6.8 mi. (11 km) beneath the surface of the Pacific Ocean

Strength of water pressure within the Challenger Deep: More than 1,000 times what is experienced at sea level

Altitude of La Rinconada, Peru: Nearly 17,000 ft. (5,200 m) above sea level

Population of La Rinconada: Approximately 30,000 people

Depth of TauTona, the world's deepest gold mine: 2.4 mi. (3.9 km)

Temperature of the rock face within TauTona: 140°F (60°C)

Did you find the truth?

(F) Mount Everest is Earth's tallest mountain.

(T) Deep within the TauTona mine, temperatures are extremely hot.

Resources

Books

Aloian, Molly. *The Andes*. New York: Crabtree Publishing, 2012.

Hyde, Natalie. *Conquering Everest*. New York: Crabtree Publishing, 2014.

Mara, Wil. *Deep-Sea Exploration: Science, Technology, and Engineering*. New York: Children's Press, 2015.

Visit this Scholastic Web site for more information on highest and lowest places:
★ www.factsfornow.scholastic.com
Enter the keywords **Highest and Lowest**

Important Words

adapt (uh-DAPT) — to change over time to fit in better with the environment

altitudes (AL-ti-toodz) — the height of objects, such as planes, clouds, or a bird, above sea level

atmosphere (AT-muhs-feer) — the mixture of gases that surrounds a planet

elevation (el-uh-VAY-shuhn) — the distance from sea level of an object or a place on the surface of the Earth

ethnic group (ETH-nik GROOP) — a population of people who share a language, culture, origin, customs, or beliefs

microbes (MYE-krohbz) — extremely small living things that can only be viewed with a microscope

migrating (MYE-grayt-ing) — moving to another area or climate at a particular time of year

probes (PROHBZ) — tools or devices used to explore or examine something

sonar (SOH-nahr) — a type of technology used on ships and submarines that sends out underwater sound waves to determine the location of objects and the distance to the bottom

trench (TRENCH) — a long, narrow hole in the ocean floor

Index

Page numbers in **bold** indicate illustrations.

About the Author

Katie Marsico graduated from Northwestern University and worked as an editor in reference publishing before she began writing in 2006. Since that time, she has published more than 200 books for children and young adults. Ms. Marsico doubts she will ever attempt to climb Mount Everest but deeply admires anyone who does.